simply knit 3

THE SIMPLY KNIT STORY CONTINUES WITH THIS THIRD COLLECTION OF HANDKNITTING PATTERNS FROM CAROL LAPIN, CC CONWAY AND NADINE SHAPIRO. AS IS THEIR HALLMARK, THESE DESIGNERS USE SIMPLE SHAPES AND FORMS TO CREATE VISUALLY INTERESTING CONTEMPORARY KNITWEAR.

LUXURIOUS LANA GROSSA YARNS—"ROYAL TWEED," "SHADOW," "BINGO," "PON PON," "DUE CHINE," "NUMERO UNO," "COOL WOOL MERINO BIG" AND "POINT"—HAVE BEEN USED THROUGHOUT THIS BOOK. THESE YARNS ARE OF THE FINEST QUALITY AND ENHANCE THE BEAUTY OF EACH DESIGN.

st. moritz

santa fe

milano

casablanca

tashkent

bangkok

veracruz

bergen

paris

berlin

milano scarf

st. moritz

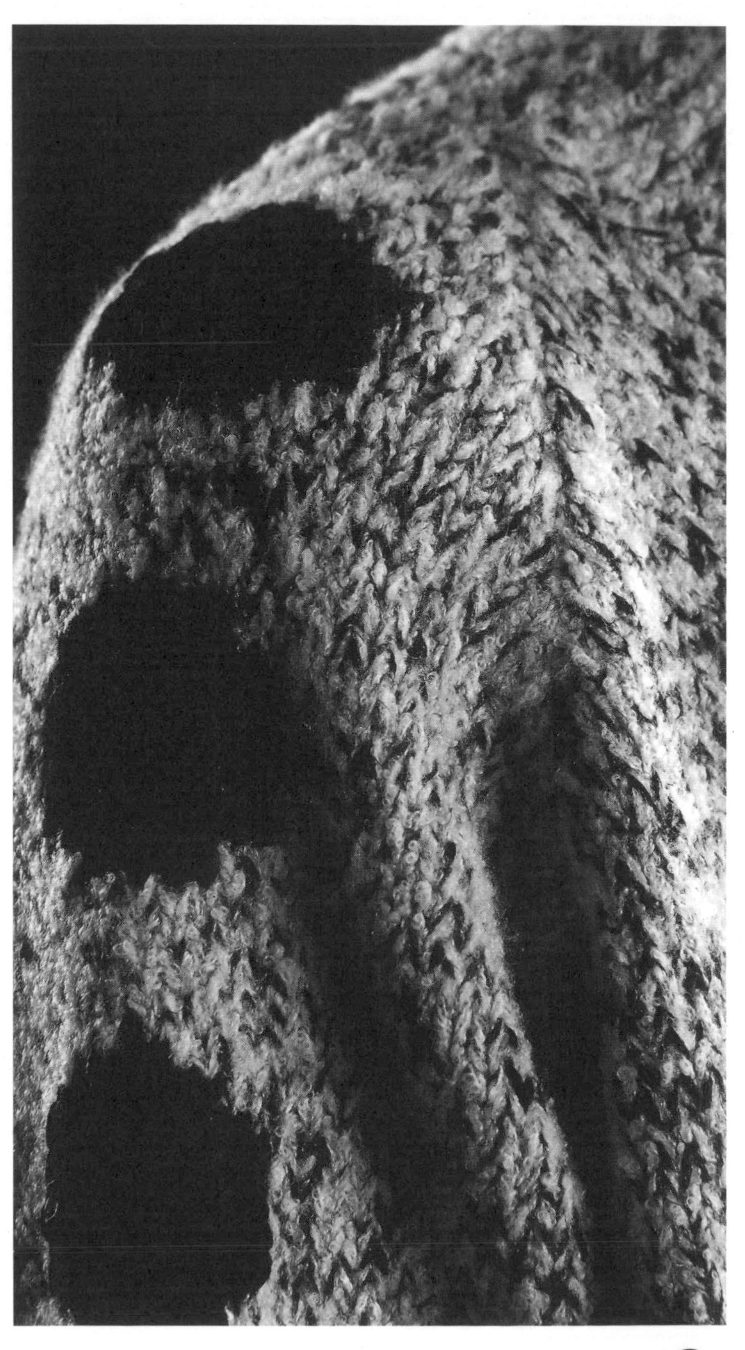

Materials

Yarn: Lana Grossa "Shadow" - 9 (10, 11) skeins Color #14; Lana Grossa "Bingo" - 2 (2, 3) skeins Color #24.
Needles: US 6 (4 mm), US 7 (4.5 mm) and US 8 (5 mm), ***or correct needles to obtain gauge.***
Accessories: Stitch holders.

Measurements

Chest: 40 (46, 52)".
Length: 21 (22, 23)".
Sleeve Length: 17 (17, 17)".

Gauge

On US 8 in st st: 17 sts and 22 rows = 4".

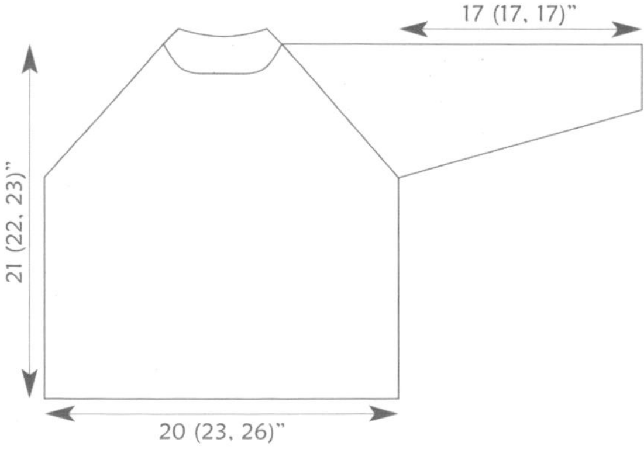

About Charts
Read odd-numbered (RS) rows from right to left, and even-numbered (WS) rows from left to right.

Notes
Each "dot" requires approx. 3 yds of yarn.

Back
With US 7 and "Shadow," CO 80 (90, 100) sts. Work 4 rows in st st beg with a knit row on RS. Change to US 8 and work 4 rows in st st. Continuing in st st, work **Chart A** (using intarsia method to work "dots" in "Bingo") over center 52 (52, 52) sts; **AND AT SAME TIME**, inc 1 st at beg and end of next row, then every 6th row 3 (3, 3) times (88 (98, 108) sts on needle). Continue without further shaping until piece measures 12½ (12½, 12½)" from CO edge, ending with RS facing for next row.

Shape Raglans
BO 6 (7, 8) sts at beg of next 2 rows, then dec 1 st at beg and end of every 2nd row 24 (26, 28) times, then **every** row 1 (3, 4) times. Place rem 26 (26, 28) sts on holder for back neck.

Front
Work same as for back up to raglan shaping.

Shape Raglans
BO 6 (7, 8) sts at beg of next 2 rows, then dec 1 st at beg and end of every 2nd row 24 (26, 28) times, then **every** row 1 (3, 4) time(s), **AND AT SAME TIME**, when there are 46 (48, 50) sts on needle, shape front neck as follows:

Shape Front Neck
While continuing to shape raglans, work to center 16 (16, 18) sts, place these on holder for front neck, and work each side separately, dec' g 1 st at neck edge every other row 4 (4, 4) times. Continue raglan shaping as for back until 2 (2, 2) sts rem for each shoulder. Place shoulder sts on holders.

Sleeves
With US 7 and "Shadow," CO 42 (42, 44) sts. Work 4 rows in st st beg with a knit row on RS. Change to US 8 and work 4 rows in st st. Continuing in st st, rep the 18 rows of **Chart B** (using intarsia method to work "dots" in "Bingo") over center 10 (10, 10) sts; **AND AT SAME TIME**, inc 1 st at beg and end of every 5th row 11 (14, 16) times (64 (70, 76) sts on needle). Work without further shaping until sleeve measures 17 (17, 17)".

Shape Raglans
Continuing **Chart B** as set, BO 6 (7, 8) sts at beg of next 2 rows, then dec 1 st at beg and end of every 2nd row 24 (26, 28) times. Place rem 4 (4, 4) sts on holder.

Finishing
Match sleeves to body along raglans and sew tog. Sew side and sleeve seams.

Neckband
With US 6 and "Shadow," RS facing, k26 (26, 28) sts from back neck holder, k4 (4, 4) sts from holder for left sleeve, k2 (2, 2) sts from holder for left front shoulder, pick up 13 (13, 13) sts down left neck edge, k16 (16, 18) sts from front neck holder, pick up 13 (13, 13) sts up right neck edge, k2 (2, 2) sts from holder for right front shoulder, and k4 (4, 4) sts from holder for right sleeve (80 (80, 84) sts on needle). Place marker, join and knit in the rnd for 3 (3, 3)". Change to "Bingo" and knit 1 rnd. Purl 3 rnds. BO.

Weave in ends. Block to finished measurements.

Chart A (Front and Back)

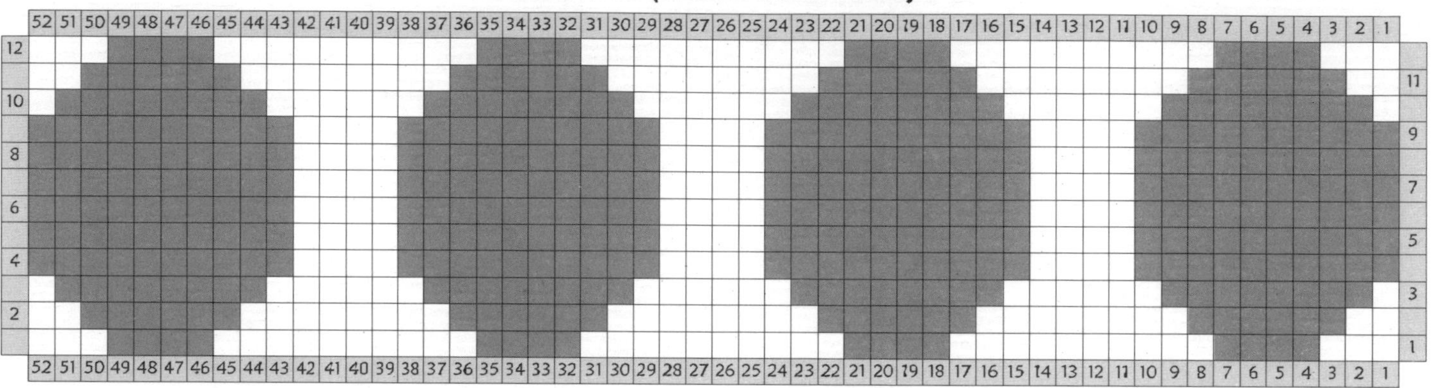

Chart B (Sleeves)

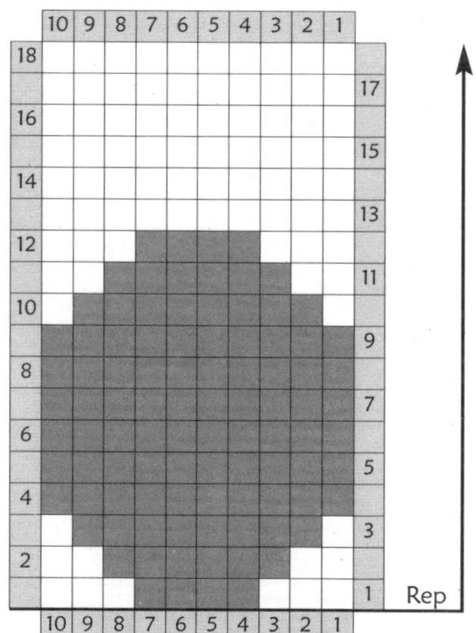

Key

- (white square) with "Shadow," k on right side rows; p on wrong side rows.
- (dark square) with "Bingo," k on right side rows; p on wrong side rows.

santa fe

Materials

Yarn: Lana Grossa "Royal Tweed" - 2 (3) skeins of Color #3; 3 (3) skeins of Color #5; 2 (2) skeins of Color #6; 2 (2) skeins of Color #12; 2 (2) skeins of Color #15; 3 (3) skeins of Color #16; 3 (3) skeins of Color #17; and 2 (2) skeins of Color #20.
Needles: US 10 (6 mm) and US 10½ (7 mm), ***or correct needles to obtain gauge.***

Measurements

Chest: 47 (57)".
Length: 24½ (26½)".
Sleeve Length: 14½ (14½)".

Gauge

On US 10½ in **Woven Stitch:** 19 sts and 30 rows = 4".

Woven Stitch (over odd no. of sts)
Row 1 (RS): *K1, sl1wyif**; rep from * to **; end sl1.
Row 2 (WS): *P1, sl1wyib**; rep from * to **; end sl1.

Back *(Worked from side to side)*
With US 10½ and Color #6, CO 114 (124) sts. Work **Woven Stitch** in the following color sequence:

14 (18) rows Color #6
4 (4) rows Color #15
10 (12) rows Color #17
14 (20) rows Color #3
4 (6) rows Color #20
12 (16) rows Color #16
10 (12) rows Color #12
4 (4) rows Color #15
10 (10) rows Color #5

Center Intarsia Section
Next Row (RS): Continuing in **Woven Stitch** as set, work 8 (8) sts Color #5, *work 8 (8) sts Color #20, work 10 (12) sts Color #5**; rep from * to ** to last 16 (16) sts; end work 8 (8) sts Color #20, work 8 (8) sts Color #5.

Work as above for 12 (12, 12) rows total, keeping continuity of color sequence on WS rows, then continue in the following color sequence:

10 (10) rows Color #5
4 (4) rows Color #15
10 (12) rows Color #12
12 (16) rows Color #16
4 (6) rows Color #20
14 (20) rows Color #3
10 (12) rows Color #17

4 (4) rows Color #15
14 (18) rows Color #6

BO.

Right Front & Left Front

(Each worked from side towards center front)

With US 10½ and Color #6, CO 114 (124) sts. Work **Woven Stitch** in the following color sequence:

14 (18) rows Color #6
4 (4) rows Color #15
10 (12) rows Color #17
14 (20) rows Color #3
4 (6) rows Color #20
12 (16) rows Color #16
10 (12) rows Color #12

BO.

Sleeves *(worked from shoulder to cuff)*

With US 10½ and Color #20, CO 84 (84) sts. Work **Woven Stitch** in the following color sequence:

8 (8) rows Color #20
16 (16) rows Color #16
12 (12) rows Color #12
20 (20) rows Color #17
22 (22) rows Color #3
10 (10) rows Color #15
16 (16) rows Color #6
6 (6) rows Color #5

AT SAME TIME, dec 1 st at beg and end of every 10th row 5 (5) times, then every 16th row 5 (5) times. Work without further shaping on rem 64 (64) sts until sleeve measures 14½ (14½)" from CO edge. BO.

Join Shoulders

With RS's facing, match front stripes to back stripes and sew shoulders tog.

Finishing

Center sleeves on shoulder seams and sew into place. Sew side and sleeve seams.

Front Band

With US 10 and Color #5, beg at bottom right, pick up 112 (122) sts up right front to shoulder seam, 28 (32) sts across back neck, and 112 (122) sts down left front to bottom left (252 (276) sts on needle). Work 6 (6) rows Color #5 in **Woven Stitch**.

Center Intarsia Section

Next Row (RS): Continuing in **Woven Stitch** as set, work 14 (14) sts Color #5, *work 8 (8) sts Color #20, work 10 (12) sts Color #5**; rep from * to ** to last 22 (22) sts; end work 8 (8) sts Color #20, work 14 (14) sts Color #5.

Work as above for 12 (12) rows total, keeping continuity of color sequence on WS rows, then work 6 (6) rows Color #5. BO.

Rolled Bottom Border

With US 10 and Color #5, RS facing, pick up 168 (192) sts along bottom of jacket, beg at front band at bottom left and working around to front band at bottom right.

Next Row (WS): Purl.
Next Row (RS): Knit.
Next Row (WS): Purl.

BO. Weave in ends. Block to finished measurements.

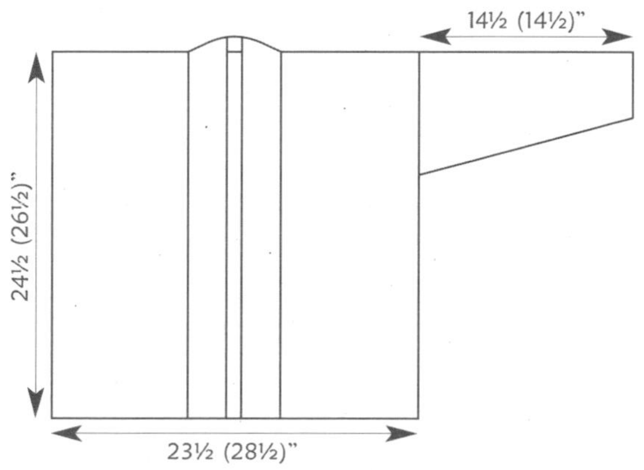

milano

Materials

Yarn: Lana Grossa "Pon Pon" - 11 (12, 13) skeins. Shown in Color #7.
Needles: US 10 (6 mm), ***or correct needle to obtain gauge.***
Accessories: Stitch holders.

Measurements

Chest: 42 (46, 50)".
Length (including fringe): 24 (25, 25)".
Sleeve Length: 16 (15½, 14)".

Gauge

On US 10 in st st: 13 sts = 4".

Back

With US 10, CO 62 (68, 72) sts. Work in st st, **AND AT SAME TIME**, inc 1 st at beg and end of row every 1 (1, 1)" 3 (3, 5) times (68 (74, 82) sts on needle). Work without further shaping until piece measures 20 (21, 21)" from CO edge, ending with RS Facing for next row.

Shape Neck

Next Row (RS): K24 (26, 30); BO 20 (22, 22); k24 (26, 30).

Working each side separately, purl 1 row. Place shoulder sts on holders.

Front

Work same as for back until piece measures 17 (18, 18)" from CO edge, ending with RS facing for next row.

Shape Neck

Next Row (RS): K28 (30, 34); k12 (14, 14) and place on holder for front neck; k28 (30, 34).

Turn, and working each side separately, dec 1 (1, 1) st at neck edge on every RS row 4 (4, 4) times. Work without further shaping on rem 24 (26, 30) sts until piece measures same as back. Place shoulder sts on holders.

Join Shoulders

With RS's facing, join shoulders using 3-needle bind-off method.

Sleeves

Place markers 8½ (9, 9)" down from shoulder seam on front and back. With US 10, RS facing, pick up 28 (30, 30) sts from marker to shoulder seam, and 28 (30, 30) sts from shoulder seam to marker (56 (60, 60) sts on needle). Work in st st, **AND AT SAME TIME**, dec 1 st at beg and end of every 4th row 12 (12, 12) times. Work without further shaping on rem 32 (36, 36) sts until piece measures 16 (15½, 14)". BO.

Neckband

With US 10, RS facing, beg at right shoulder seam, pick up 22 (23, 24) sts along back neck edge, 13 (13, 13) sts down left neck edge, k12 (14, 14) sts from front neck holder, pick up 13 (13, 13) sts up right neck edge (60 (63, 64) sts on needle). Place marker, join and knit in the rnd until neckband measures 2½ (2½, 2½)". Purl 3 rnds. BO in purl.

Finishing

Sew side and sleeve seams. Cut 10" lengths of yarn to make fringe and attach to each st along bottom edge of sweater. Weave in ends. Block to finished measurements.

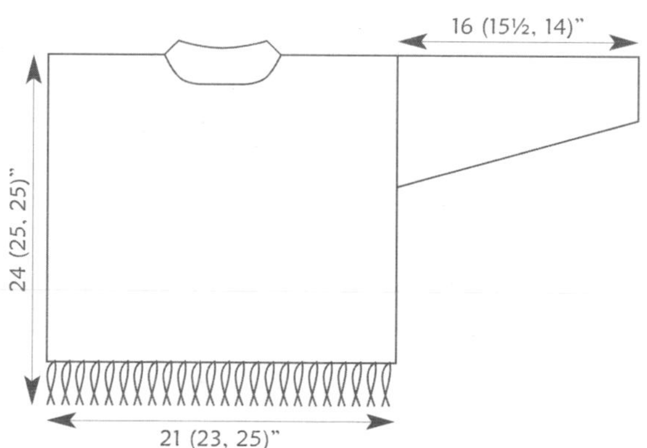

milano scarf

Materials
Yarn: Lana Grossa "Pon Pon Print" - 2 (3) skeins. Shown in Color #202.
Needles: US 13 (9 mm), ***or correct needle to obtain gauge.***

Measurements
Width: 4 (4)".
Length (not including fringe): 52 (72)".

Gauge
On US 13 in **Seed Stitch**: 13 sts = 4".

Seed Stitch
Every Row: *K1, p1**; rep from * to **; end k1.

Scarf
With US 13 CO 13 (13) sts loosely. Work in **Seed Stitch** until scarf measures 52 (72)". BO in pattern.

Finishing
Make fringe and attach to ends as desired.

casablanca

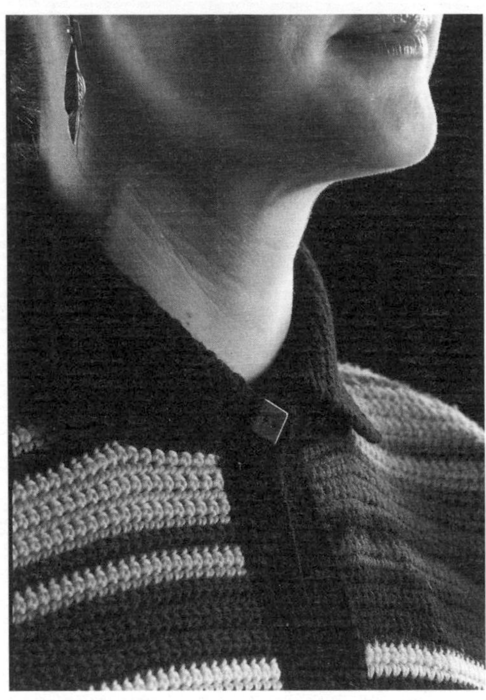

Materials

Yarn: Lana Grossa "Cool Wool Merino Big" - 5 (7) skeins of Color A (#627); 4 (5) skeins of Color B (#625); 2 (3) skeins of Color C (#623); 3 (4) skeins each of Color D (#649); Color E (644); Color F (#603); and Color G (#646).
Needles: Size F crochet hook, ***or correct size to obtain gauge.***
Accessories: One ½" button and snap.

Measurements

Chest: 40 (44)".
Length: 22 (23¾)".
Sleeve Length: 17½ (17½)".

Gauge

With Size F crochet hook: 20 sc = 4".

Stripe Sequence

Stripe 1: 6 rows Color B
Stripe 2: 2 rows Color G
Stripe 3: 2 rows Color B
Stripe 4: 6 rows Color G
Stripe 5: 2 rows Color F
Stripe 6: 2 rows Color G
Stripe 7: 6 rows Color F
Stripe 8: 2 rows Color E
Stripe 9: 2 rows Color F
Stripe 10: 6 rows Color E
Stripe 11: 2 rows Color D
Stripe 12: 2 rows Color E
Stripe 13: 6 rows Color D
Stripe 14: 2 rows Color A
Stripe 15: 2 rows Color D
Stripe 16: 6 rows Color A
Stripe 17: 2 rows Color C
Stripe 18: 2 rows Color B
Stripe 19: 6 rows Color C
Stripe 20: 2 rows Color B
Stripe 21: 2 rows Color C

Stripe Row

Sc in 1st sc from hook and in each sc across row. Ch 1. Turn.

Back

With Color A, ch 100 (110).

Foundation Row (RS): Sc in 2nd ch from hook and in each ch across row (99 (109) sc). Ch 1. Turn.

Work **Stripe Row** 5 (5) times until you have a total of 6 (6) rows in Color A. Continue to rep **Stripe Row**, working **Stripe 1-21 (1-21)** and **Stripe 1-13 (1-16)** of **Stripe Sequence**. Fasten off.

Left Front
With Color A, ch 49 (55)

Foundation Row (RS): Sc in 2nd ch from hook and in each ch across row (48 (54) sc). Ch 1. Turn.

Work **Stripe Row** 5 (5) times until you have a total of 6 (6) rows in Color A. Continue to rep **Stripe Row**, working **Stripe 13-21 (13-21)**, **Stripe 1-21 (1-21)** and **Stripe 1-4 (1-7)** of **Stripe Sequence**, **AND AT SAME TIME**, when piece measures 19 (20½)" and **Stripe 19 (1)** is complete, continuing in **Stripe Sequence** as set, with RS facing, sc 40 (44) sts. Ch 1. Turn. Dec 1 sc at neck edge on every RS row 7 (8) times. Continue without further shaping on rem 33 (36) sc until stripe sequence is complete. Fasten off.

Right Front
With Color A, ch 49 (55).

Foundation Row (RS): Sc in 2nd ch from hook and in each ch across row (48 (54) sc). Ch 1. Turn.

Work **Stripe Row** 5 (5) times until you have a total of 6 (6) rows in Color A. Continue to rep **Stripe Row**, working **Stripe 7-21 (7-21)** and **Stripe 1-19 (1-21 + Stripe 1)** of **Stripe Sequence**, **AND AT SAME TIME**, when piece measures 19 (20½)" and **Stripe 13 (16)** is complete, continuing in **Stripe Sequence** as set, with RS facing, skip first 8 (10) sc, attach yarn to 9th (11th) sc and work rem 40 (44) sts. Ch 1. Turn. Dec 1 sc at neck edge on every RS row 7 (8) times. Continue without further shaping on rem 33 (36) sc until stripe sequence is complete. Fasten off.

Sleeves
With Color A, ch 49 (55).

Foundation Row (RS): Sc in 2nd ch from hook and in each ch across row (48 (54) sc). Ch 1. Turn.

Work **Stripe Row** 5 (5) times until you have a total of 6 (6) rows in Color A. Continue to rep **Stripe Row**, (working **Stripe 13-21 (13-21)** and **Stripe 1-19 (1-19)** of **Stripe Sequence** for *left sleeve*; and **Stripe 6-21 (6-21)** and **Stripe 1-12 (1-12)** for *right sleeve*), **AND AT SAME TIME**, inc 1 sc at beg and end of every 4th row 22 (23) times. Continue without further shaping on 92 (100) sc until sleeve measures 17½ (17½)". Fasten off.

Finishing
Sew shoulder seams tog. Place markers 9 (10)" down from shoulder seam on front and back and sew sleeves to body between markers. Sew sleeve and side seams.

Front Borders
With Color A, RS facing, work 1 row of sl st crochet along front edge.

Next Row (RS): Sc in top loop of each sl st to end. Ch 1. Turn.

Work 3 more rows of sc through both loops. Fasten off.

Collar
With Color A, RS facing, work 32 (34) sl sts up right neck edge (including top of right border), 30 (30) sl sts across back of neck, and 32 (34) sts down left neck edge (including top of left border). Fasten off. With RS, facing, reattach Color A 3 sts in from front edge. Sc approx. 86 (92) sts, ending 3 sts in from end of opposite front border.

Next Row (WS): Work sc, dec'g 14 (16) sc evenly across row.

Work until collar measures 4 (4)". Fasten off. Sew snap to inside at top of front border. Sew button to outside. Weave in ends. Block to finished measurements.

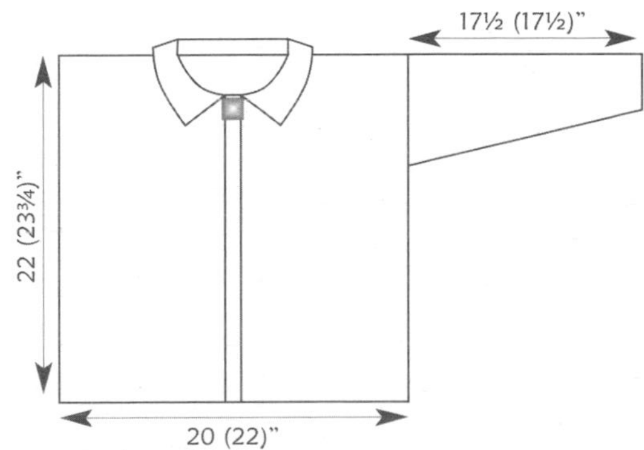

tashkent

Materials
Yarn: Lana Grossa "Due Chine" - 15 (17) skeins. Shown in Color #401.
Needles: 16" and 24" circular US 10 (6 mm) and 32" circular US 10½ (7 mm), ***or correct needles to obtain gauge.***
Accessories: Stitch holders.

Measurements
Chest: 44 (48)".
Length: Approx. 23½ (23½)" (measured from bottom point and excluding fringe).
Sleeve Length: 17½ (17½)".

Gauge
On US 10½ in st st: 13 sts and 18 rows = 4".

Back

With US 10½, CO 2 (2) sts.

Work **Chart**, inc' g at beg and end of every row as shown, twisting cable on Row 19, then every 12th row thereafter. Work through row 34 (38), then work without further shaping on 70 (76) sts, continuing cable as set, until piece measures approx. 23½ (23½)", ending after working Row 5 of cable. Place center 20 (20) sts on holder for back neck, and 25 (28) sts for each shoulder on separate holders.

Front

Work same as for back until piece is 12 rows less than back.

Shape Neck

Next Row (RS): K30 (33), place next 10 (10) sts on holder for front neck, k30 (33).

Turn, and working each side separately, dec 1 st at neck edge every other row 5 (5) times. Work without further shaping on rem 25 (28) sts until piece measures same as back. Place shoulder sts on separate holders.

Join Shoulders

With RS's facing, join shoulders using 3-needle bind-off method.

Sleeves

With US 10, CO 34 (34) sts.

Row 1 (WS): *P2, k2**; rep from * to ** to last 2 sts; end p2.
Row 2 (RS): *K2, p2**; rep from * to ** to last 2 sts; end k2.

Rep Rows 1 and 2 above until piece measures 4" from CO edge, ending with RS facing for next row. Change to US 10½ and work in st st, **AND AT SAME TIME**, inc 1 st at beg and end of every 4th row 8 (10) times, then every 6th row 3 (4) times (56 (62) sts on needle). Work without further shaping until piece measures 17½ (17½) from CO edge. BO.

Finishing

Place markers 10" down from shoulder seam on front and back and sew sleeve to body between markers. Sew side and sleeve seams.

Neck

With 16" circular US 10, RS facing, beg at left shoulder seam, pick up 11 (11) sts down left neck edge; p1, k8, p1 from front neck holder; pick up 11 (11) sts up right neck edge; p2, k2, p2, k8, p2, k2, p2 from back neck holder (52 (52) sts on needle). Join, and working in the rnd, set up neck as follows:

Next Row: K2, p2, k2, p2, k2, p2, k8, p2, k2, p2, k2, p2, k2, p2, k2, p2, k8, p2, k2, p2.

Keeping continuity of cable pattern, rep this row until neck measures 3 (3)". BO in pattern.

Fringe

Cut yarn into 12" lengths and attach fringe to bottom of garment as shown on schematic, using 3 strands for each fringe.

Weave in ends. Block to finished measurements.

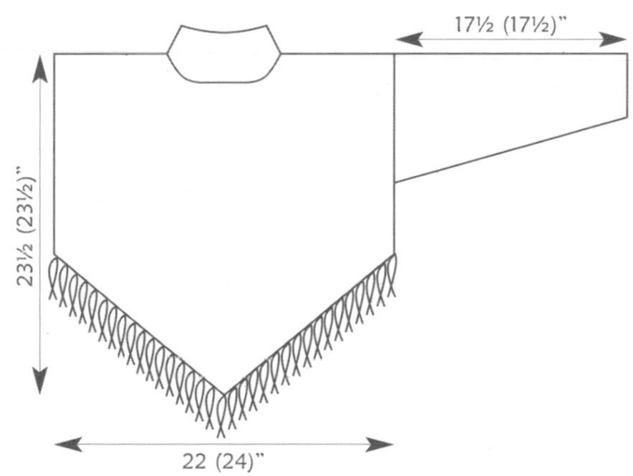

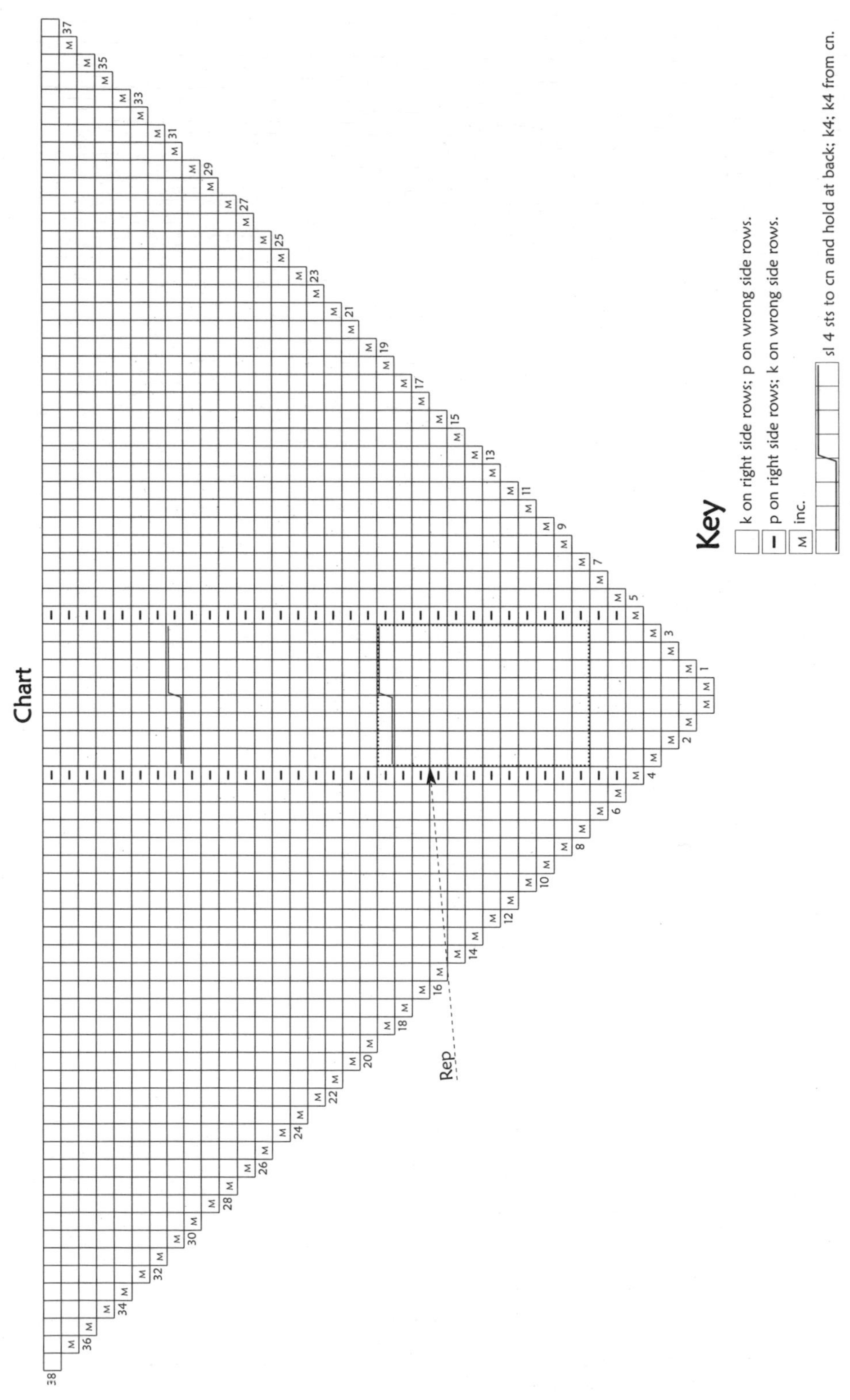
Chart
Rep
Key
k on right side rows; p on wrong side rows.
p on right side rows; k on wrong side rows.
M inc.
sl 4 sts to cn and hold at back; k4; k4 from cn.

bangkok

Materials

Yarn: Lana Grossa "Royal Tweed" - 14 (15, 17) skeins of Color A (#20); Lana Grossa "Bingo" - 1 (1, 1) skein each of Color B (#7); Color C (#51); Color D (#69) and Color E (#24).
Needles: US 6 (4 mm) and US 7 (4.5 mm), ***or correct needles to obtain gauge.***
Accessories: Stitch holders. Four fasteners.

Measurements

Chest: 44 (47, 50)".
Length: 26 (26½, 27)".
Sleeve Length: 18 (17½, 17)".

Gauge

On US 7 in garter st: 17 sts and 34 rows = 4".

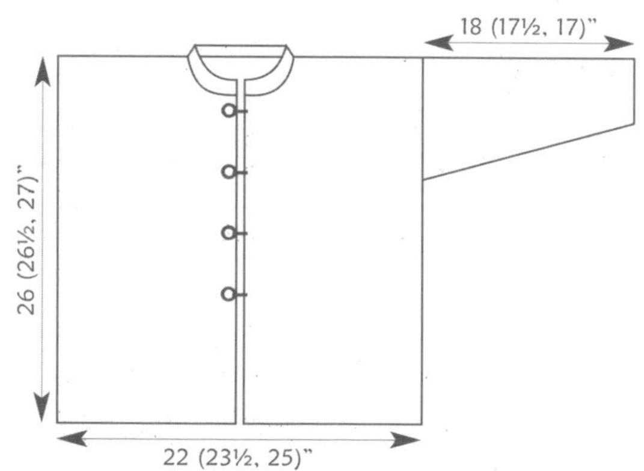

About Charts

Read odd-numbered (RS) rows from right to left and even-numbered (WS) rows from left to right.

Back

With US 7 and Color A, CO 96 (102, 108) sts. Work in garter st for 17 (17, 17½)", ending with RS facing for next row.

Shape Armhole

BO 6 (6, 6) sts at beg of next 2 rows. Work without further shaping on rem 84 (90, 96) sts until piece measures 26 (26½, 27)" from CO edge. Place 28 (30, 32) sts on holder for right shoulder, 28 (30, 32) sts on another holder for back neck, and 28 (30, 32) sts on another holder for left shoulder.

Left Front

With US 7 and Color A, CO 49 (52, 55) sts. Work in garter st for 17 (17, 17½)", ending with RS facing for next row.

Shape Armhole

BO 6 (6, 6) sts at beg of next row. Work without further shaping on rem 43 (46, 49) sts until piece measures 23 (23½, 24)" from CO edge.

Shape Neck

BO 6 (6, 7) sts at neck edge once, 3 (3, 3) sts 3 (2, 2) times and 2 (2, 2) sts 0 (2, 2) times. Work without further shaping on rem 28 (30, 32) sts until piece measures 26 (26½, 27)" from CO edge. Place shoulder sts on holder.

Right Front

Work same as for left front, reversing shaping.

Join Shoulders

With RS's facing, join shoulders using 3-needle bind-off method.

Sleeves

With US 7 and Color A, RS facing, pick up 40 (42, 42) sts from underarm to shoulder seam and 40 (42, 42) sts from shoulder seam to underarm (80 (84, 84) sts on needle). Work in garter st for 1½ (1½, 1½)". Continue in garter st, **AND AT SAME TIME**, dec 1 st at beg and end of every 6th row 15 (16, 16) times. Work without further shaping on rem 50 (52, 52) sts until piece measures 16½ (16, 15½)". Place CUFF sts on holder.

Finishing

Sew side seams.

Collar

With US 6 and Color E, pick up 22 (23, 24) sts up right neck edge, k28 (30, 32) sts from back neck holder, and pick up 22 (23, 24) sts down left neck edge (72 (76, 80) sts on needle). Knit back and forth as follows:

Next Row (WS): With Color E, p36 (38, 40), m1, p36 (38, 40).

Work the 9 rows of **Chart**.

Next Row (WS) (Turning Ridge): With Color B, knit.

With Color B, work 11 rows in st st. BO loosely. Turn to inside and sew down.

Cuffs

Place sleeve cuffs sts onto US 6, and with Color E, k25 (26, 26), m1, k25 (26, 26) (51 (53, 53) sts on needle). With Color E, purl 1 row.

Work the 9 rows of **Chart**.

Next Row (WS) (Turning Ridge): With Color B, knit.

With Color B, work 11 rows in st st. BO loosely. Sew sleeve seam. Turn cuff to inside and sew down.

Sew fasteners to fronts, spaced approx. 5" apart. Weave in ends. Block to finished measurements.

Chart

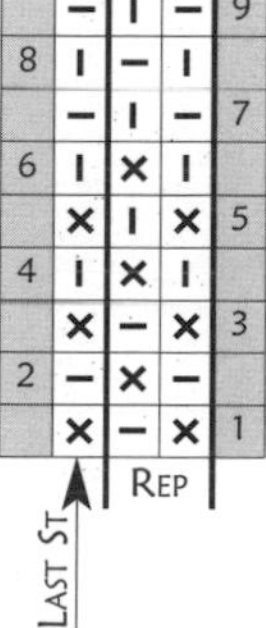

Key

—	Color B - "Bingo" #7
×	Color C - "Bingo" #51
I	Color D - "Bingo" #69

veracruz

Materials

Yarn: Lana Grossa "Numero Uno Tweed" - 3 (4, 5) skeins of Color A (#310); 2 (3, 4) skeins each of Color B (#318) and Color C (#311). Lana Grossa "Numero Uno Fancy" - 2 (3, 4) skeins of Color D (#607).
Needles: Double-pointed US 3 (3.25 mm); 32" circular US 5 (3.75 mm) and US 6 (4 mm), ***or correct needles to obtain gauge.***

Measurements

Chest: 40 (49, 56)".
Length: 19 (23, 26)".

Gauge

On US 6 in garter st: 20 sts = 4".
On US 6 in **Basic Square:** 15 sts = 1½" x 1½"; 17 sts = 1¾" x 1¾"; 19 sts = 2" x 2".

Basic Square Pattern

Worked on 15 (17, 19) sts on US 6 in color indicated.

Row 1 (WS): Knit to last st, p1.
Row 2 (RS): Sl1 kwise, knit to center 3 sts, sl1, k2tog, psso, knit to last st, p1 (mark this side so you know it's the RS).
Row 3 (and all rem WS rows): Sl1 kwise, knit to last st, p1.

Rep Rows 2 and 3 until 5 sts rem.

Next Row (RS): Sl1 kwise, sl1, k2tog, psso, p1.
Next Row (WS): Sl1 kwise, p2tog, psso.

Leave last rem st on needle (if working square for Left Front) or leave open and remove from needle (if working square for Right Front). Turn square to RS ready to beg new square. *If last square in row, pull yarn through last rem st for both Right Front and Left Front squares.*

Back

With US 6 and Color C, CO 100 (120, 140) sts. Working in garter st throughout, work **Stripes 1-7** of **Back *Stripe Sequence*** .

Shape Armhole

Continuing **Back *Stripe Sequence***, BO 7 (9, 11) sts at beg of next 2 rows, then dec 1 st at beg and end of every RS row 5 (5, 5) times. Continue through **Stripe 12** on rem 76 (92, 108) sts. Work 10 (12, 14) rows of Stripe 13.

Shape Neck

Next Row (RS) (Row 11 (13, 15) of Stripe 13): K21 (24, 27), BO 34 (44, 54) sts for back neck, k21 (24, 27).

Working each side separately, work last row as follows:

Next Row (WS) (Row 12 (14, 16) of Stripe 13): Work last row of Stripe 13. Place shoulder sts on holders.

Left Front

Note: Refer to **Left Front *Color Chart*** and **Left Front *Squares Sequence*** for colors and sequences.

Row 1

Square 1: With US 6 and color indicated, work **Basic Square Pattern**, ending with 1 st rem on needle. Turn to RS. Tilt square so diagonal line in middle of square slants from bottom right to top left.

Squares 2-7: With last st of previous square still on needle, with color indicated, pick up 6 (7, 8) sts along left edge of previous square and CO 8 (9, 10) sts (15 (17, 19) sts on needle). Work **Basic Square Pattern,** ending with 1 st on needle. Turn to RS. *If last square in row, pull yarn through last rem st.*

Row 2

Square 8: With color indicated, CO 8 (9, 10) sts and pick up 7 (8, 9) sts along top of right-most square in previous row (15 (17, 19) sts on needle). Work **Basic Square Pattern**, ending with 1 st on needle. Turn to RS.

Squares 9-14: With last st of previous square still on needle, with color indicated, pick up 7 (8, 9) sts along left edge of previous square and 7 (8, 9) sts along top of square below (15 (17, 19) sts on needle). Work **Basic Square Pattern**, ending with 1 st on needle. Turn to RS. *If last square in row, pull yarn through last rem st.*

Rows 3-7 (Squares 15-49)

Work in same manner as in Row 2.

Shape Armhole

Row 8

Square 50: With RS facing and color indicated, pick up 8 (9, 10) sts along top of Square 44.

Row 1 (WS): Sl1 kwise, k to last st, p1.
Row 2 (RS): Sl1 kwise, sl1, k1, psso, k to last st, p1.

Rep Rows 1-2 above until 3 sts rem.

Row 3 (WS): Sl1 kwise, k1, p1.
Row 4 (RS): Sl1 kwise, p2tog.
Row 5 (WS): Sl1 kwise, p1.
Row 6 (RS): Sl1 kwise, k1, psso. Leave last rem st on needle.

Squares 51-55: Work in same manner as Squares 9-14 in Row 2.

Rows 9-11 (Squares 56-70)

Work in same manner as in Row 2.

Row 12

Squares 71-73: Work in same manner as in Row 2.

Shape Neck

Square 74: With last st of Square 73 still on needle, with RS facing and color indicated, pick up 7 (8, 9) sts along left side of Square 73, pick up 7 (8, 9) sts along top of Square 69 (15 (17, 19) sts on needle).

Row 1 (WS): Sl1 kwise, k to last st, p1.
Row 2 (RS): Sl1 kwise, k to last 3 sts, k2tog, p1.

Rep Rows 1-2 above until 3 sts rem.

Row 3 (WS): Sl1 kwise, k1, p1.
Row 4 (RS): Sl1 kwise, p2tog.
Row 5 (WS): Sl1 kwise, p1.
Row 6 (RS): K2tog. Pull yarn through last rem st.

Row 13
Squares 75-77: Work in same manner as in Row 2.

Right Front

Note: Refer to **Right Front *Color Chart*** and **Right Front *Squares Sequence*** for colors and sequences.

Row 1
Square 1: With US 6 and color indicated, work **Basic Square Pattern**, ending with 1 st rem; leave this st open and remove from needle. Turn square to RS and tilt so diagonal line in middle of square slants from bottom left to top right.

Squares 2-7: With color indicated, CO 7 (8, 9) sts, pick up 7 (8, 9) sts along right edge of previous square, place rem st from previous square onto needle (15 (17, 19) sts on needle). Work **Basic Square Pattern**, ending with 1 st rem; leave this st open and remove from needle. Turn to RS. *If last square in row, pull yarn through last rem st.*

Row 2
Square 8: With color indicated, pick up 7 (8, 9) sts along top of left-most square in previous row and CO 8 (9, 10) sts (15 (17, 19) sts on needle). Work **Basic Square Pattern**, ending with 1 st rem; leave this st open and remove from needle. Turn to RS.

Squares 9-14: With color indicated, pick up 7 (8, 9) sts along top of square below and 7 (8, 9) sts along right side of previous square, place rem st from previous square onto needle (15 (17, 19) sts on needle). Work **Basic Square Pattern**, ending with 1 st rem; leave this st open and remove from needle. Turn to RS. *If last square in row, pull yarn through last rem st.*

Rows 3-7 (Squares 15-49)
Work in same manner as in Row 2.

Shape Armhole
Row 8
Square 50: With RS facing and color indicated, pick up 8 (9, 10) sts along top of Square 44.

Row 1 (WS): Sl1 kwise, k to last st, p1.
Row 2 (RS): Sl1 kwise, k to last 3 sts, k2tog, p1.

Rep Rows 1-2 above until 3 sts rem.

Row 3 (WS): Sl1 kwise, k1, p1.
Row 4 (RS): Sl1 kwise, p2tog.
Row 5 (WS): Sl1 kwise, p1.
Row 6 (RS): K2tog. Leave last rem st open and remove from needle.

Squares 51-55: Work in same manner as Squares 9-14 in Row 2.

Rows 9-11
Work in same manner as in Row 2.

Row 12
Squares 71-73: Work in same manner as in Row 2.

Shape Neck
Square 74: With RS facing and color indicated, pick up 7 (8, 9) sts along top of Square 69 and 7 (8, 9) sts along right side of Square 73; place last rem st of Square 73 on needle (15 (17, 19) sts on needle).

Row 1 (WS): Sl1 kwise, k to last st, p1.
Row 2 (RS): Sl1 kwise, sl1, k1, psso, k to last st, p1.

Rep Rows 1-2 above until 3 sts rem.

Row 3 (WS): Sl1 kwise, k1, p1.
Row 4 (RS): Sl1 kwise, p2tog.
Row 5 (WS): Sl1 kwise, p1.
Row 6 (RS): Sl1 kwise, k1, psso. Pull yarn through last rem st.

Row 13
Squares 75-77: Work in same manner as in Row 2.

Finishing

Block pieces, stretching back slightly (if necessary) so height of stripes matches height of squares on fronts.

Join Shoulders

With US 6 and Color A, RS facing, pick up 21 (24, 27) sts along left front shoulder. Places sts from holder for back left shoulder onto another US 6. With WS's facing, join using 3-needle bind-off method. Rep for right shoulder.

Join Side Seams

With US 6 and Color A, RS facing, pick up 7 (9, 11) sts in each square along left side of left front between bottom and underarm (49 (63, 77) sts on needle). With another US 6, pick up 7 (9, 11) sts in each stripe along left back (49 (63, 77) sts on needle). With WS's facing, join using 3-needle bind-off method. Rep for right side seam.

Armhole Border

With US 5 and Color A, RS facing, pick up 7 (9, 11) sts in each square along armhole edge from underarm up to shoulder seam, 1 (1, 1) st in shoulder seam, and 7 (9, 11) sts in each stripe down armhole edge to underarm (99 (127, 155) sts on needle).

Next Row (WS): Knit.
Next Row (RS): Purl.

BO in knit. Sew border tog at underarm. Rep for right armhole, picking up sts in reverse direction.

Front Borders

With US 5 and Color A, RS facing, pick up 7 (9, 11) sts in each square along left front edge (77 (99, 121) sts on needle).

Next Row (WS): Knit.
Next Row (RS): Purl.

BO in knit. Rep for right front.

Bottom Border

With US 5 and Color A, RS facing, pick up 52 (59, 66) sts along bottom of right front, 100 (120, 140) sts along bottom of back, and 52 (59, 66) sts along bottom or left front (204 (238, 272) sts on needle).

Next Row (WS): Knit.
Next Row (RS): Purl.

BO in knit.

Neck

With US 5 and Color A, RS facing, pick up 80 (88, 96) sts around neck edge.

Row 1 (WS): Knit.
Row 2 (RS): Purl.

Row 3 (WS): Using intarsia method, p10 (11, 12) sts each in Color B, Color C, Color D, Color A, Color B, Color C, Color D, and Color A.
Row 4 (RS): Continuing color sequence as set, purl.

Rep Rows 3-4 above once more. BO in knit.

Tie

With double-pointed US 3, pick up 3 sts in top corner of Square 70 on left front.

Every Row: K3; without turning, slide sts to other end of needle.

Rep row above until tie measures 8". Rep in Square 70 of right front.

Weave in ends. Block to finished measurements.

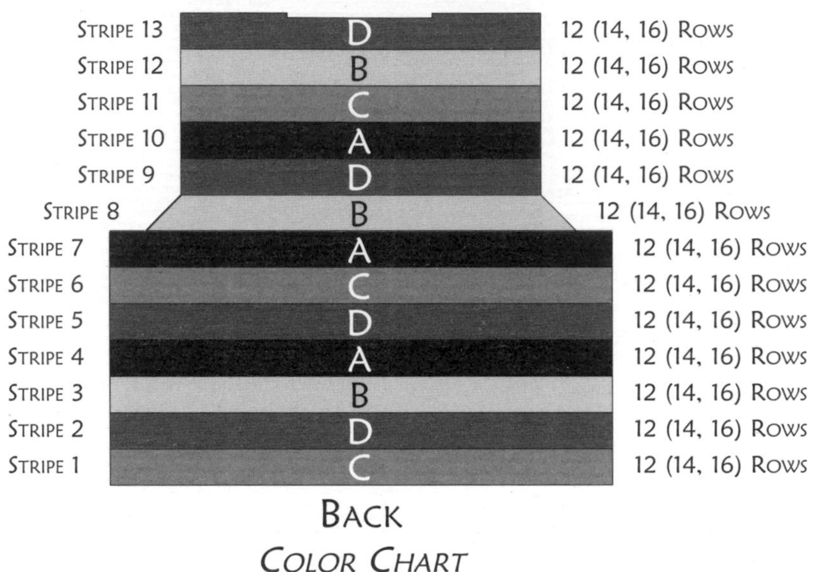

Back
Color Chart

Color Key

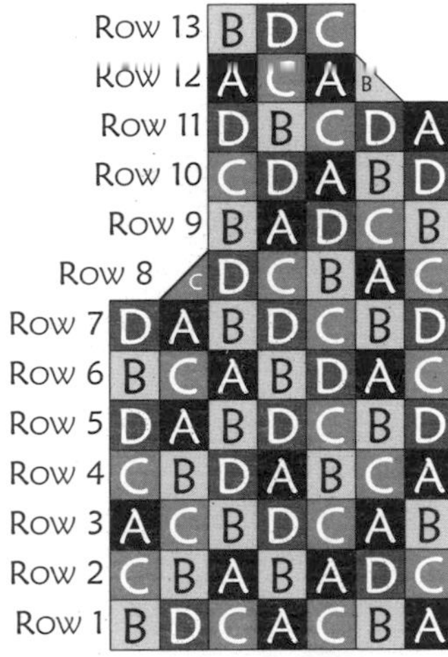

RIGHT FRONT
COLOR CHART

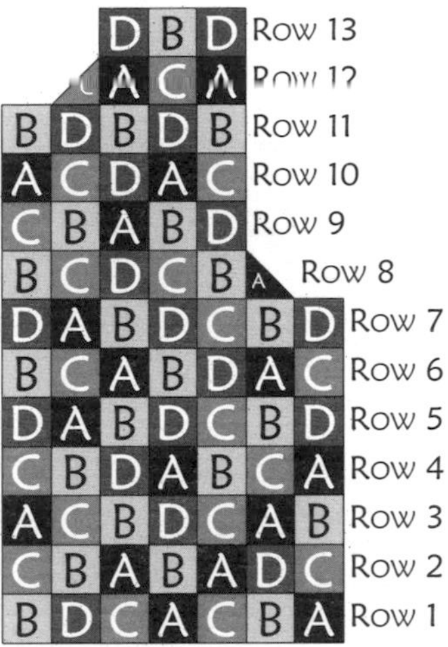

LEFT FRONT
COLOR CHART

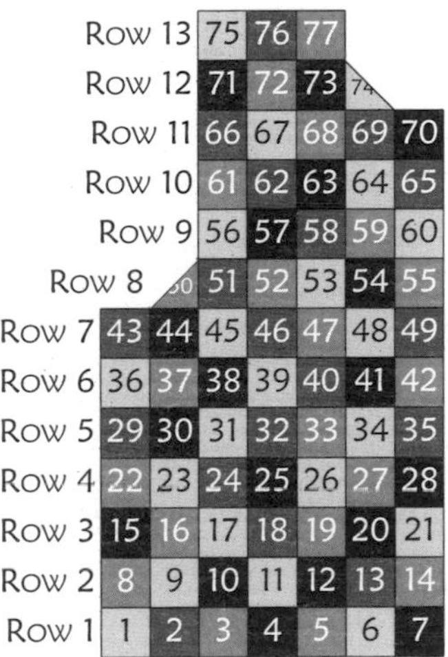

RIGHT FRONT
SQUARES SEQUENCE

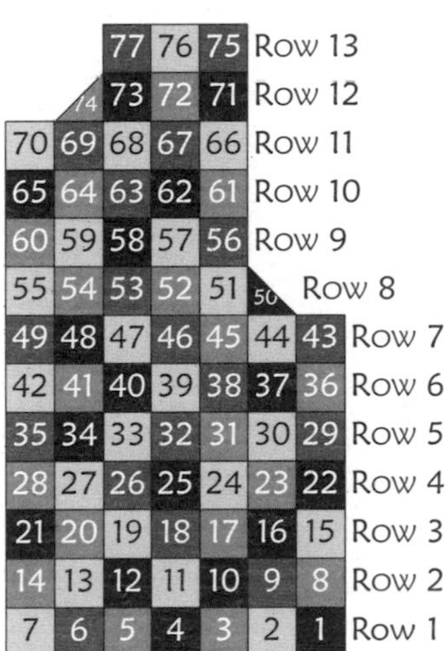

LEFT FRONT
SQUARES SEQUENCE

A NUMERO UNO TWEED (#310)
B NUMERO UNO TWEED (#318)
C NUMERO UNO TWEED (#311)
D NUMERO UNO FANCY (#607)

COLOR KEY

bergen

Materials

Yarn: Lana Grossa "Due Chine" - 5 (6, 7, 8) skeins of Color A; 7 (8, 9, 10) skeins of Color B; and 2 (2, 3, 3) skeins of Color C. Shown in Color A, #406; Color B, #410 and Color C, #412.
Needles: 16" and 32" circular US 10 (6 mm), ***or correct needles to obtain gauge.***
Accessories: Stitch holders.

Measurements

Chest: 40 (43, 46, 49)".
Length: 20 (21, 22, 23)".
Sleeve Length: 17½ (17½, 18½, 18½)".

Gauge

On US 10 in st st: 14 sts and 20 rows = 4".

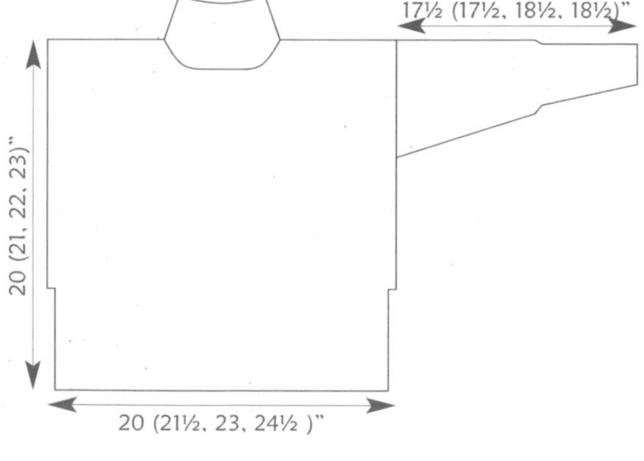

Ribbing Pattern for Body (Multiple of 6)

Row 1 (RS): ([K4, p2] 14 (15, 16, 17) times.
Row 2 (WS): ([K2, p4] 14 (15, 16, 17) times.

Rep Rows 1-2.

Ribbing Pattern for Sleeves (Multiple of 6 +2)

Row 1 (RS): *P2, k4**; rep from * to **; end p2.
Row 2 (WS): *K2, p4**; rep from * to **; end k2.

Rep Rows 1-2.

Back

With US 10 and Color A, CO 84 (90, 96, 102) sts. Work in **Ribbing Pattern for Body** for 7 (7, 8, 8)", ending with RS facing for next row. Change to Color B and work as follows:

Next Row (RS): ([K4, k2tog] 14 (15, 16, 17) times).

Continue in st st on rem 70 (75, 80, 85) sts until piece measures 20 (21, 22, 23)" from CO edge, ending with RS facing for next row.

Next Row (RS): K22 (24, 26, 28) sts and place on holder for right shoulder, k26 (27, 28, 29) sts and place on another holder for back neck, k22 (24, 26, 28) sts and place on another holder for left shoulder.

Front

Work same as for back until piece measures 18 (18½, 19, 19½)" from CO edge, ending with RS facing for next row.

Next Row (RS): K30 (32, 34, 36) sts and place on holder, k10 (11, 12, 13) sts and place on on holder for front neck, k30 (32, 34, 36) sts.

Turn, and working each side separately, dec 1 st at neck edge every row 8 (8, 8, 8) times. Continue without further shaping on rem 22 (24, 26, 28) sts until same length as back. Place shoulder sts on separate holders.

Join Shoulders

With RS's facing, join shoulders using 3-needle bind-off method.

Sleeves

Place marker 8½ (8½, 9½, 9½)" down from shoulder seams on both back and front. With US 10 and Color B, pick up 29 (29, 33, 33) sts along armhole edge from marker to shoulder seam and 29 (29, 33, 33) sts from shoulder seam to other marker (58 (58, 66, 66) sts on holder). Work in st st, **AND AT SAME TIME**, dec 1 st at beg and end of every 4th row 10 (10, 11, 11) times. Work without further shaping on rem 38 (38, 44, 44) sts until piece measures 8 (8, 9, 9)", ending with RS facing for next row.

Change to Color A and work **Ribbing Pattern for Sleeves** for 8 (8, 8, 8)". Change to Color C and continue ribbing for 6 more rows. BO.

Neck

With 16" circular US 10 and Color B, beg at right shoulder seam, k26 (27, 28, 29) sts from back neck holder, pick up 9 (11, 13, 15) sts down left neck edge, k10 (11, 12, 13) sts from front neck holder, pick up 9 (11, 13, 15) sts up right neck edge (54 (60, 66, 72) sts on needle). Change to Color C, join, and work in the rnd as follows, centering rib pattern on neckband:

Rnds 1-8: *K4, p2**; rep from * to ** to end of rnd.

Rnds 9-27: *P4, k2**; rep from * to ** to end of rnd.

BO in pattern.

Finishing

Sew side and sleeve seams. Weave in ends. Block to finished measurements.

paris

Materials

Yarn: Lana Grossa "Point" - 4 (5, 6) skeins each of MC and CC. Shown in MC, #18 and CC, #19.
Needles: 24" circular US 5 (3.75 mm), US 6 (4.5 mm) and US 9 (5.5 mm), ***or correct needles to obtain gauge.***
Accessories: Stitch holders. Two ¾" buttons.

Measurements

Chest: 40 (44, 48)".
Length: 23 (24, 25)".

Gauge

On US 6 in st st: 22 sts and 28 rows = 4".

Lace Pattern (Multiple of 6 + 1)
Row 1 (RS): K1, *yo, k1, k3tog, k1, yo, k1**; rep from * to **.
Row 2 (WS): P1, *k5, p1**; rep from * to **.

Rep Rows 1-2.

Border Pattern (Multiple of 12 + 1)
Note: *Stitch count changes from row to row.*
Row 1 (WS): Knit.
Rows 2, 4, 6 & 8 (RS): K1, ssk *k9, sl 2 pwise, k1, p2sso**; rep from * to ** to last 12 sts; end k9 k2tog, k1 (113 (125, 137) sts on needle).
Rows 3, 5 7 (WS): K1, *p1, k4, (k1, yo, k1 in same st), k4**; rep from * to ** to last 2 sts; end p1, k1 (135 (147, 159) sts on needle).

Work Rows 1-8 once.

Back

Make Lace Bottom

With US 9 and CC, CO 109 (121, 133) sts and knit one row. Work **Lace Pattern** until piece measures 6½ (6½, 6½)" from CO edge. Change to US 7 and MC and knit 1 row, inc'g 4 (4, 4) sts evenly across row (113 (125, 137) sts on needle). Leave sts on needle.

Make Border Pattern

With US 6 and MC, CO 135 (147, 159) sts. Work the 8 rows of **Border Pattern**, ending after working a RS row (113 (125, 137) sts on needle). Leave sts on needle.

Join Lace Bottom to Border Pattern

With US 6 and MC, RS's facing, place needle with **Lace Bottom** behind needle with **Border Pattern** and knit each st of **Lace Bottom** tog with each st of **Border Pattern**.

Work in st st, **AND AT SAME TIME**, dec 1 st at beg and end of every 10th row 3 (5, 7) times. Continue on rem 107 (115, 123) sts until piece measures 13 (14, 15)" from CO edge of **Lace Bottom**.

Shape Underarms

BO 10 (12, 14) sts at beg of next 2 rows (87 (91, 95) sts on needle), BO 2 (2, 2) sts at beg of next 4 (6, 8) rows (79 (79, 79) sts on needle), then dec 1 st at beg and end of every RS row 10 (10, 10) times (59 (59, 59 sts on needle).

ALSO AT SAME TIME, when piece measures 16½ (17½, 18½)" from CO edge of **Lace Bottom**, shape neck as follows:

Shape Neck

Next Row (RS): K24 (24, 24) sts, BO 11 (11, 11) sts, k24 (24, 24) sts.

Turn, and working each side separately, dec at neck edge 2 (2, 2) sts 3 (3, 3) times, then 1 (1, 1) st 4 (4, 4) times. Work without further shaping on rem 14 (14, 14) sts until piece measures 23 (24, 25)" from CO edge of **Lace Bottom**. Place shoulder sts on holders.

Front

Work same as for back.

Join Shoulders

With RS's facing, join shoulders using 3-needle bind-off method.

Finishing

Sew side seams.

Armband edging

With US 5 and CC, RS facing, beg at underarm, pick up approx. 166 (170, 175) sts around armhole. Place marker, join and work as follows:

Row 1 (WS): Knit.
Row 2 (RS): Purl.
Row 3 (WS): Knit.

BO in purl.

Neck Edging

With US 5 and CC, RS facing, beg at right shoulder seam, pick up approx. 220 (230, 240) sts around neck edge. Place marker, join and work as follows:

Row 1 (WS): Knit.
Row 2 (RS): Purl.
Row 3 (WS): Knit.

BO in purl.

Sew 2 or 3 buttons vertically below center of front neck. Weave in ends. Block to finished measurements.

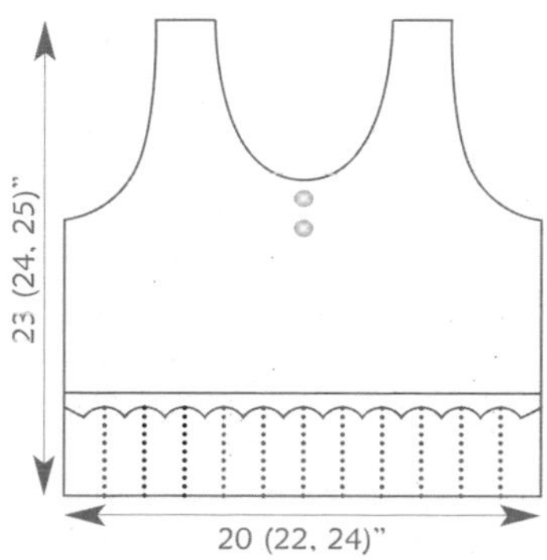

berlin

Materials

Yarn: Lana Grossa "Cool Wool Merino Big" - 13 (14, 16) skeins. Shown in Color #653.
Needles: US 5 (3.75 mm) and US 7 (4.5 mm), ***or correct needles to obtain gauge.***
Accessories: Stitch holders.

Measurements

Chest: 40 (44, 48)".
Length: 20 (20, 22)".
Sleeve Length: 17½ (17½, 17½)".

Gauge

On US 7 in **Chart A or B**: 24 sts and 29 rows = 4".

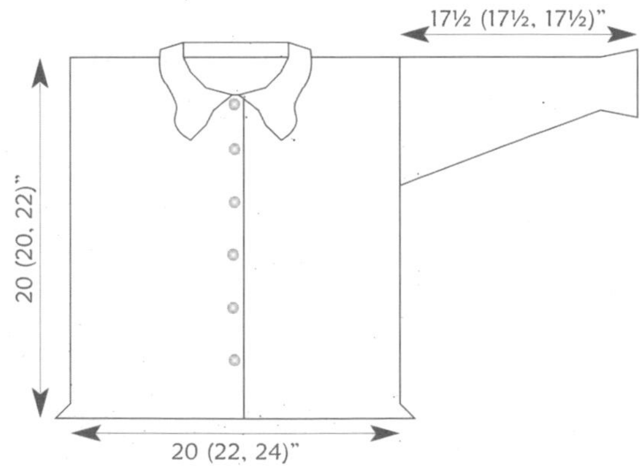

Make Buttonholes

Row 1 (RS): Work 3 sts, BO 2 sts, work to end of row.
Row 2 (WS): Work to last 3 sts, CO 2, work last 3 sts.

Work Rows 1-2 for each buttonhole.

Back

With US 5, CO 212 (228, 240) sts.

Row 1 (RS): Knit.
Row 2 (WS): Purl.
Row 3 (RS): *([K2tog] twice), ([p2tog] twice)**; rep from * to ** (106 (114, 120) sts rem).

Change to US 7 and rep the 8 rows of **Chart B, AND AT SAME TIME**, inc 1 st at beg and end of every 4th row 8 (10, 12) times, incorporating inc'd sts into pattern. Work without further shaping on 122 (134, 144) sts until piece measures 20 (20, 22)" from CO edge, ending with RS facing for next row.

Shape Neck

Next Row (RS): Work 45 (50, 54) sts, BO 32 (34, 36) sts for back neck, work 45 (50, 54) sts.

Working each side separately, purl 1 row. Place shoulder sts on holders.

Right Front

With US 5, CO 120 (140, 160) sts.

Row 1 (RS): Knit.
Row 2 (WS): Purl.
Row 3 (RS): *([K2tog] twice), ([p2tog] twice)**; rep from * to ** (60 (70, 80) sts rem).

Change to US 7 and rep the 8 rows of **Chart A, AND AT SAME TIME**, inc 1 st at **end** of every 4th row 8 (10, 12) times, incorporating inc'd sts into pattern.

ALSO AT SAME TIME, while continuing to work **Chart A**, when piece measures 3 (3, 2½)" from CO edge, and RS faces for next row, **Make Buttonholes** spaced 2½ (2½, 3)" apart and placing last buttonhole ½" from top of buttonhole band. When piece measures 17½ (17½, 19½)" from CO edge, ending with RS facing for next row, shape neck as follows:

Shape Neck

Continuing **Chart A** as set, BO at neck edge 7 (10, 12) sts once, 4 (4, 7) sts twice, 3 (3, 3) sts twice, 0 (2, 2) sts twice, and 1 (1, 1) st twice. Work without further shaping on rem 45 (50, 54) sts until piece measures 20 (20, 22)" from CO edge. Place shoulder sts on holders.

Left Front

With US 5, CO 120 (140, 160) sts.

Row 1 (RS): Knit.
Row 2 (WS): Purl.
Row 3 (RS): *([K2tog] twice), ([p2tog] twice)**; rep from * to ** (60 (70, 80) sts rem).

Change to US 7 and rep the 8 rows of **Chart B, AND AT SAME TIME**, inc 1 st at **beg** of every 4th row 8 (10, 12) times, incorporating inc'd sts into pattern. Work without further shaping on 68 (80, 92) sts until piece measures 17½ (17½, 19½)" from CO edge, ending with RS facing for next row, shape neck as follows:

Shape Neck

Continuing **Chart B** as set, BO at neck edge 7 (10, 12) sts once, 4 (4, 7) sts twice, 3 (3, 3) sts twice, 0 (2, 2) sts twice, and 1 (1, 1) st twice. Work without further shaping on rem 45 (50, 54) sts until piece measures 20 (20, 22)" from CO edge. Place shoulder sts on holders.

Join Shoulders

With RS's facing, join shoulders using 3-needle bind-off method.

Right Sleeve

With US 5, CO 132 (132, 140) sts.

Row 1 (RS): Knit.
Row 2 (WS): Purl.
Row 3 (RS): *([K2tog] twice), ([p2tog] twice)**; rep from * to ** (66 (66, 70) sts rem).

Change to US 7 and work in **Chart B**, **AND AT SAME TIME,** ***dec*** 1 st at beg and end of every 3rd row 7 (7, 7) times (52 (52, 56) sts on needle), then work 8 (8, 8) rows without shaping, then ***inc*** at beg and end of every 4th row 11 (11, 11) times (74 (74, 78) sts on needle), then ***inc*** at beg and end of every 3rd row 18 (18, 18) times (110 (110, 114) sts on needle). Work without further shaping until sleeve measures 17½ (17½, 17½)" from CO edge. BO.

Left Sleeve

Work same as for right sleeve, substituting **Chart A** for Chart B.

Collar

With US 7, RS facing, pick up 25 (28, 35) sts up right neck edge, 34 (36, 38) sts along back neck edge, and 25 (28, 35) sts down left neck edge (84 (92, 108) sts on needle. Rep the 8 rows of **Chart C**, **AND AT SAME TIME**, inc 1 st at beg and end of every 3rd row 7 (9, 8) times, incorporating inc' d sts into pattern (98 (110, 124) sts on needle), ending with RS facing for next row. Change to US 5.

Next Row (RS): K5 (6, 9) sts; knit into front and back of every st (inc) to last 5 (6, 9) sts; end k5 (6, 9).
Next Row (WS): Purl.

BO.

Finishing

Center sleeves on shoulder seams and sew into place. Sew side sand sleeve seams. Sew buttons opposite buttonholes.

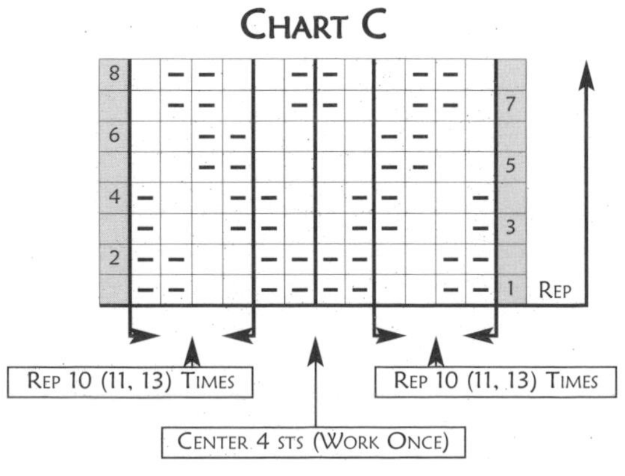

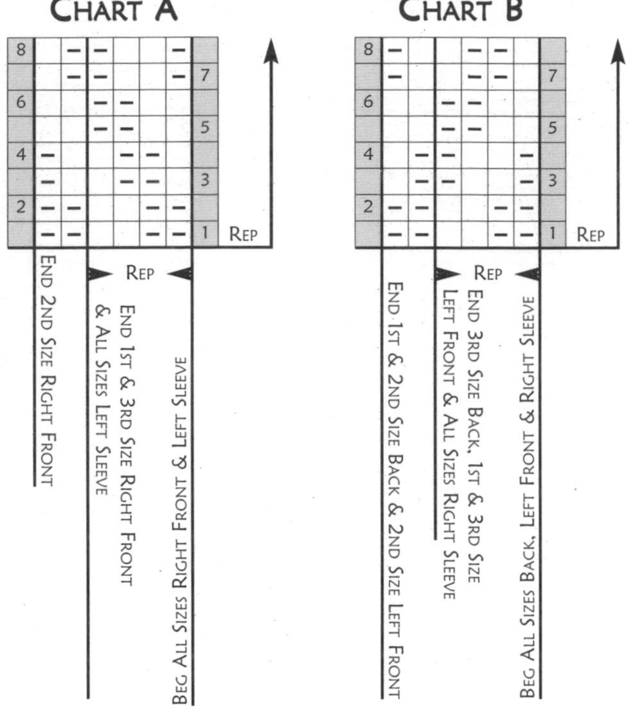

Key

- ☐ k on right side rows; p on wrong side rows.
- – p on right side rows; k on wrong side rows.

Abbreviations

ALT = alternate
BEG = beginning
BO = bind off
CC = contrast color
CH = chain (crochet)
CN = cable needle
CO = cast on
DEC = decrease(ing)
GS = garter stitch
INC = increase(ing)
K = knit
K1B = knit through back loop
K2TOG = knit 2 sts together
K2TOGTBL = knit 2 sts together through back loop
M1 = make 1 st (inc) - lift the running thread between the st just worked and the next st and knit into the back of this loop
MC = main color
P = purl
P2SSO = pass 2 slipped sts over
P2TOG = purl 2 sts together
PATT = pattern
PSSO = pass slipped stitch over st just knitted
REM = remaining
REP = repeat
RND = round
RS = right side
SC = single chain (crochet)
SL = slip
SL1WYIB = with yarn in back, slip 1 st purlwise
SL1WYIF = with yarn in front, slip 1 st purlwise
SSK = sl 2 sts (one at a time) knitwise; with left-hand needle, knit these two sts tog through front of sts
ST(S) = stitch(es)
ST ST = stockinette stitch
TBL = through back loop
TOG = together
WS = wrong side
YB (yarn back) = take yarn to back of work
YF (yarn forward) = bring yarn to front of work
YO = yarn over needle

A SELECTION OF LANA GROSSA YARNS CAN BE FOUND AT THESE FINE STORES:

ALABAMA
Huntsville - Yarn Expressions
800-283-8409

ALASKA
Anchorage - LANA GROSSA AT Knitting Frenzy
800-478-8322

ARKANSAS
Little Rock - LANA GROSSA AT The Handworks Gallery
501-664-6300

CALIFORNIA
Alameda - Yarn!
510-522-9276
Burbank - LANA GROSSA AT Unwind
818-786-4906
Campbell - The Rug & Yarn Hut
408-871-0411
Glendale - Emmaline's
818-547-5747
Half Moon Bay - Fengari
650-726-2550
Healdsburg - A Good Yarn
707-473-9705
Los Altos - LANA GROSSA AT Uncommon Threads
650-941-1815
Los Angeles - LANA GROSSA AT Jennifer Knits
310-471-8733
Los Angeles - LANA GROSSA AT Knit Cafe
323-658-5648
Los Angeles - Knitter's Studio
323-655-6487
Los Angeles - LANA GROSSA AT Black Sheep Knitting
323-464-2253
Menlo Park - LANA GROSSA AT The Knitter's Studio
650-322-9200
Monterey - LANA GROSSA AT Monarch Knitting and Quilt
831-647-9276
Nevada City - Meadow Farm Yarn Studio
530-470-8862
Oakland - LANA GROSSA AT Article Pract
510-652-7435
Orinda - Infinit Possibilities
925-254-1125
Petaluma - Knitterly
707-762-9276
Redondo Beach - LANA GROSSA AT L'Atelier
310-540-4440
Rocklin - Filati
800-398-9043
Rohnert Park - Elf Hand Knitwerks
707-584-8635
San Carlos - Creative Hands
650-591-0588
San Francisco - Atelier Yarns
415-771-1550
San Francisco - Greenwich Yarns
415-567-2535
San Francisco - LANA GROSSA AT ImagiKnit
415-621-6642
San Francisco - Urban Knitting Studio
415-552-5333
Saratoga - Knitting Arts
408-867-5010
Santa Clarita - LANA GROSSA AT Simply Knitting
661-513-0955
Santa Monica - Wild Fiber
310-458-2748
Sebastopol - Knitting Workshop
707-824-0699
Sherman Oaks - Needle World
818-784-2442
St. Helena - Gale Laurence Studio
707-967-9500
Studio City - LANA GROSSA AT La Knitterie Parisienne
800-228-9927
Tahoe City - Three Dog Knits
530-583-0001
Tarzana - Knit Purl & Co.
818-774-9971
Tracy - K2 Knits Yarn Salon
209-830-7604
Valley Village - LANA GROSSA AT Stitch Cafe
818-980-1234
Van Nuys - A Major Knitwork
818-787-2659
Walnut Creek - Fashion Knit
925-943-3994
Westlake Village - LANA GROSSA AT Rockin Rose
818-597-1002
Woodland Hills - LANA GROSSA AT A Yarn for All Seasons
818-999-2720
Mail Order Only - Yarn Market
www.yarnmarket.com

COLORADO
Loveland - Woolen Treasures
970-613-0556

CONNECTICUT
Avon - Wool Connection
800-933-9665
Bethel - A Stitch in Time
203-748-1002
New Milford - The Village Sheep, LLC
860-354-5442
New Branford - Yarns Yarns Yarns
203-488-7370
Stamford - Knit Together
203-324-9276
Stratford - Janet Kemp, LLC
203-386-9276
Torrington - Hither & Yarn
860-489-9276

FLORIDA
Pompano Beach - The Gifting Tree
954-975-5722

GEORGIA
Kennesaw - The Knitting Emporium
770-421-1919
Roswell - Cast-On Cottage
888-998-9019

IDAHO
Twin Falls - Sheep to Shawl
208-735-8425

ILLINOIS
Chicago - We'll Keep You In Stitches
312-642-2540
Lake Forest - Keweenaw Shepherd
847-295-9524
Long Grove - I'd Rather Be Knitting
847-634-9276
Northbrook - 3 Bags Full
847-291-9933

INDIANA
Fort Wayne - Cass Street Depot
888-420-2292
Indianapolis - Mass Ave Knit Shop
800-675-8565
Terre Haute - River Wools
812-238-0090
Valparaiso - Sheep's Clothing
219-462-1700

MAINE
Camden - Stitchery Square
207-236-9773

MARYLAND
Baltimore - Woolworks
410-337-9030
Bethesda - Yarns International
800-927-6728
Potomac - Yarn Dog
301-765-6296
Rockville - Wool Winders
240-632-9276

MASSACHUSETTS
Amherst - The Creative Needle
413-549-6106
Boston - Windsor Button
617-482-4969
Brookline - A Good Yarn
617-731-4900
Cambridge - Woolcott & Co.
617-547-2837
Concord - Needle Arts of Concord
978-371-0424
Gardner - Wicker & Wool
978-632-8573
Jamaica Plain - Circles Salon, LLC
617-524-5500
Lenox - Colorful Stitches
800-413-6111
Lexington - LANA GROSSA AT Wild & Woolly Studio
781-861-7717
Littleton - The World in Stitches, Inc.
978-486-8330
Milton - Snow Goose Yarns
617-698-1190
N. Grafton - Classic Yarns of Grafton
508-839-6111
Northhampton - Webs
800-367-9327
Walpole - Dee's Nimble Needles
508-668-8499

MICHIGAN
Ada - LANA GROSSA AT Clever Ewe
616-682-1545
Ann Arbor - Knit A Round Yarn Shop
734-998-3771
Cadillac - Knitter's Nest
231-775-9276
Clare - Apple Tree Lane
989-386-2552
Grosse Point - The Wool & the Floss
313-882-9110
Holland - Lizzie Ann's Wool Co., Inc.
616-399-4740
Lansing - Threadbear Fiber Arts Studio
517-703-9276
Marquette - Town Folk Gallery
906-225-9010
Plymouth - Old Village Yarn Shop
734-451-0580
Rochester - LANA GROSSA AT Skeins on Main
248-656-9300
Sterling Heights - Indigo Rose Yarn
248-650-6056

MINNESOTA
Brainerd - Freyja's
218-824-6005
Excelsior - LANA GROSSA AT Coldwater Collaborative
952-401-7501
Grand Marais - That Little Red House
218-475-9950

Grand Rapids - Yarnworks
218-326-9339
Hibbing - Knitting Knight
218-262-5764
Minneapolis - Creative Fibers
612-927-8307
Minneapolis - Linden Hill Yarns
612-929-1255
Minneapolis - **Lana Grossa at** Needlework Unlimited
888-925-2454
Minnetonka - Skeins
952-939-4166
North St. Paul - K2 P2
612-812-5663
Osseo - **Lana Grossa at** Amazing Threads
763-391-7700
Rosemount - Yarn Garage
651-423-2590
St. Paul - **Lana Grossa at** Three Kittens Yarn Shoppe
651-457-4969
St. Paul - **Lana Grossa at** The Yarnery
651-222-5793
White Bear Lake - **Lana Grossa at** A Sheepy Yarn Shoppe
800-480-5462

MONTANA
Missoula - Kaye's Creative Knitting
406-721-5223

NEW HAMPSHIRE
Exeter - **Lana Grossa at** Charlotte's Web
603-778-1417
Laconia - The Yarn Shop & Fibres
603-528-1221
Nashua - Ewe'll Love It
603-578-2630

NEW JERSEY
Englewood - Handknits
201-567-9885
Lambertville - **Lana Grossa at** Simply Knit
609-397-7101
Pennington - Woolly Lamb
609-730-9800

NEW YORK
New York - String
212-288-9276
New York - Knit New York
212-387-0707
New York - Yarn Connection
212-684-5099
Northport - Three Black Sheep
631-262-9276
Pelham - Wool Works
914-738-0104
Rochester - **Lana Grossa at** The Village Yarn Shop
585-454-6064
Valley Stream - Able Charted Consultants, Inc.
516-561-7200

NORTH CAROLINA
Asheville - Yarn Paradise
828-274-4213
Black Mountain - Wilde & Wooly Yarn Shop
828-669-0600
Charlotte - Charlotte Yarn
704-373-7442
Greensboro - Yarns, Etc.
336-370-1233
Huntersville - Knit One, Stitch Too
704-655-9558
Raleigh - **Lana Grossa at** Great Yarns
800-810-0045

OHIO
Avon - French Creek Fiber Arts
440-934-1236
Cincinnati - Knit Happens!
513-871-9276
Cleveland - Fine Points, Inc.
216-229-6644
Columbus - Wolfe Fiber Arts
614-487-9980
Defiance - The Fifth Stitch
419-782-0991
Lakewood - River Color Studio
216-228-9276
Toledo - FiberWorks Knitting & Weaving
419-389-1821
Westlake - Knitting Garden, Inc.
440-250-5648
Woodmere - The Knitting Room
216-464-8450

OREGON
Ashland - **Lana Grossa at** Web-sters
800-482-9801
Bandon - The Wool Company
541-347-3912
Carlton - Woodland Woolworks
800-547-3725
Coos Bay - My Yarn Shop
541-266-8230
Portland - Lint
503-226-8500
Portland - **Lana Grossa at** Yarn Garden
503-239-7950

PENNSYLVANIA
Chadd's Ford - Garden of Yarn Co.
888-226-5648
Chambersburg - The Yarn Basket
888-976-2758
Duncansville - Victoria's House of Needle Arts
800-574-2033
East Berlin - Manning's Handweaving Studio
717-624-2223
Lancaster - **Lana Grossa at** Oh Susanna Yarns
717-393-5146
Ligonier - Kathy's Kreations
724-238-9320
Monroeville - Bonnie Knits
412-856-7033
Philadelphia - Rosie's Yarn Cellar
215-977-9276
Philadelphia - **Lana Grossa at** Tangled Web
215-242-1271
Sewickley - Yarns Unlimited
412-741-8894
West Reading - **Lana Grossa at** Yarn Gallery
613-373-1622
Willow Street - Legacy Yarn
717-464-7575

RHODE ISLAND
Providence - **Lana Grossa at** A Stitch Above
800-949-5648
Tiverton - Sakonnet Purls
401-624-9902

SOUTH CAROLINA
Columbia - Girls in Purls
803-407-4340
Greenville - The Needle Tree
864-235-6060

TENNESSEE
Brentwood - Threaded Bliss & Yarn
615-370-8717
Chattanooga - Genuine Pearl
423-267-7335
Memphis - Yarn to Go
901-454-4118
Memphis - Yarniverse
901-818-0940
Memphis - The Yarn Studio
901-276-5442
Nashville - Angel Hair Yarn Co.
615-269-8833

TEXAS
Austin - **Lana Grossa at** Hill Country Weavers
512-707-7396
Houston - Nimblefingers
713-722-7244

VIRGINIA
Alexandria - Knit Happens, Inc.
703-836-0039
Alexandria - Springwater Workshop
703-549-3634
Burke - The Yarn Barn
800-762-5274
Charlottesville - It's a Stitch
434-973-0331
Falls Church - Aylin's Woolgatherer
703-573-1900
Richmond - Knitting Basket, Ltd.
804-282-2909
Virginia Beach - Knit Wits
757-498-6600
Virginia Beach - **Lana Grossa at** Ewe Knit & Yarns
757-498-4590
Williamsburg - Knitting Sisters
757-258-5005

VERMONT
Essex Junction - Kaleidoscope Yarn
802-288-9200

WASHINGTON
Bainbridge Island - Churchmouse Yarns & Teas
206-780-2686
Bellevue - Parkside Wool Co.
425-455-2138
Bellevue - Skeins
425-452-1248
Kennewick - Sheep's Clothing
509-734-2484
Seattle - Hilltop Yarn & Needlepoint
206-282-5330
Seattle - Tricoter
206-328-6505
Seattle - The Weaving Works
888-524-1221
Tacoma - Fibers, Etc.
253-531-3257

WISCONSIN
Appleton - Jane's Knitting Hutch
920-954-9001
Delafield - **Lana Grossa at** Knitting Ark
262-646-2464
Fond Du Lac - The Knitting Room
920-906-4800
Green Bay - Monterey Yarn
920-884-5258
Milwaukee - **Lana Grossa at** Ruhama's Yarn & Needlepoint
414-332-2660
Neenah - Yarns by Design
888-559-2767

CANADA
London, Ontario - Needles & Pins, Inc.
519-642-3445

"Lana Grossa at . . ." stores carry a wide range of Lana Grossa yarns.

Editorial Director **David Codling**

Editor & Graphic Design **Gregory Courtney**

Assistant to the Editor **Diane Brown**

Designers **Carol Lapin, CC Conway & Nadine Shapiro**

Photography **Kathryn Martin**

Garments Modeled by **Michelle Rich**

Makeup & Hair Styling **Kira Lee**

Cloting Stylist **Betsy Westman**

Buttons **Muench Buttons** (www.muenchyarns.com)

Color Reproduction & Printing **Global Interprint, Inc.**

Published and Distributed By **Unicorn Books and Crafts, Inc.** (www.unicornbooks.com)

Printed in Hong Kong

ISBN
1-893063-09-7

1 2 3 4 5 6 7 8 9 10

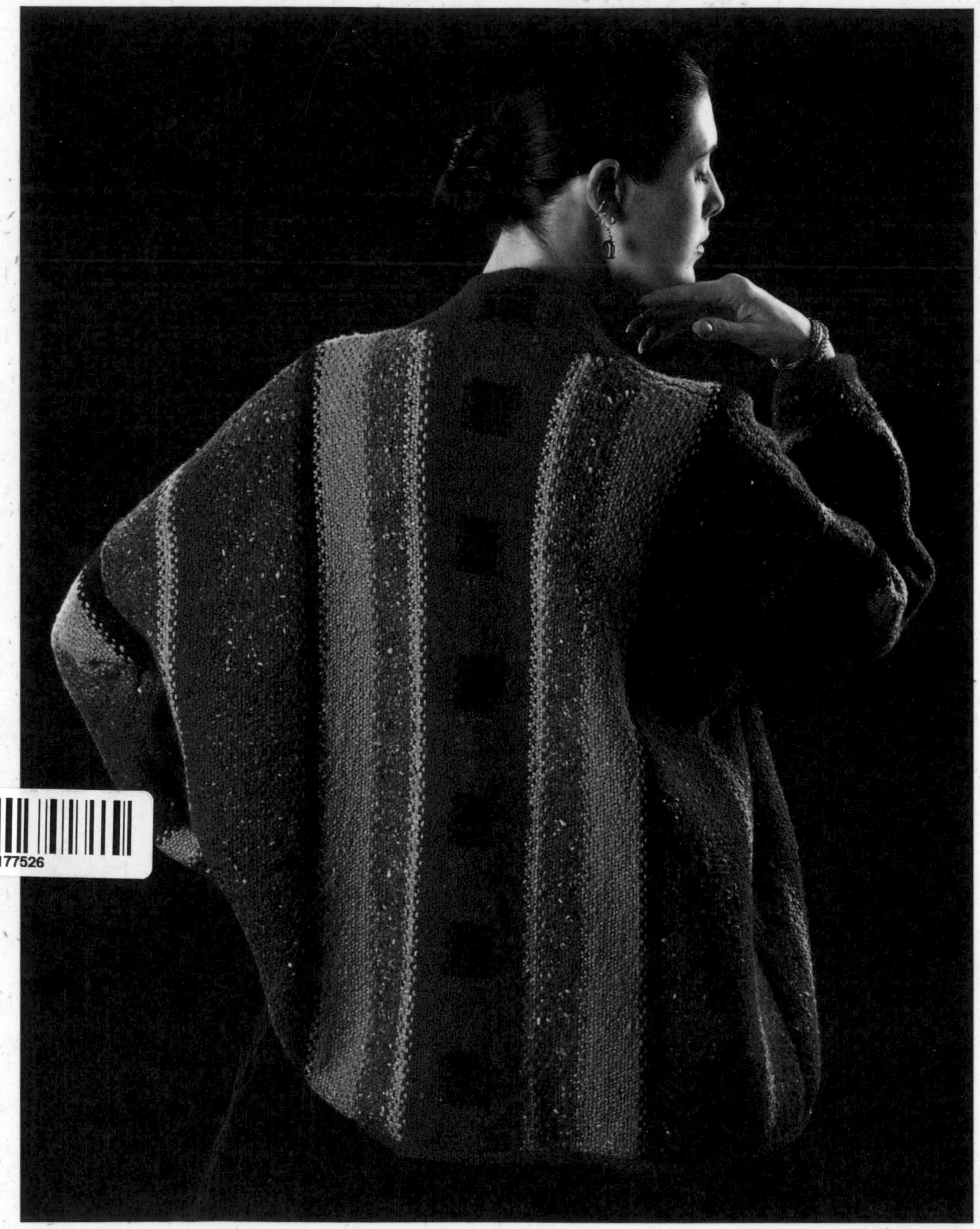

simply knit 3

ISBN 1-893063-09-7